The Air's Accomplices

The Air's Accomplices

Poems

——— ∞ ———

BRENDAN GALVIN

[signature: Brendan Galvin]

Louisiana State University Press

Baton Rouge

Published by Louisiana State University Press
Copyright © 2015 by Brendan Galvin
All rights reserved
Manufactured in the United States of America
LSU Press Paperback Original
FIRST PRINTING

Designer: Mandy McDonald Scallan
Typeface: Corda

Thanks to the editors of the following magazines, in which some of the poems in this col-
lection were first published: *Agni, Atlantic Monthly, Crazyhorse, Georgia Review, Gettysburg
Review, Hotel Amerika, Image, Meridian, New Hibernia Review,* the *New Yorker, Plume,
Post Road, Sewanee Review, Shenandoah, The Southern Review, Tar River Poetry, Virginia
Quarterly Review.*

"An Evel Knievel Elegy" appeared in *Literature to Go* and *The Compact Bedford Introduction
to Literature,* both edited by Michael Meyer (Bedford/St. Martin's, 2010).

Library of Congress Cataloging-in-Publication Data
Galvin, Brendan.
  [Poems. Selections]
  The air's accomplices : poems / Brendan Galvin.
    pages cm
  ISBN 978-0-8071-5903-3 (pbk. : alk. paper) — ISBN 978-0-8071-5905-7 (epub) — ISBN
  978-0-8071-5904-0 (pdf) — ISBN 978-0-8071-5906-4 (mobi)
  I. Title.
  PS3557.A44A6 2015
  811'.54—dc23

                                                                          2014024591

The paper in this book meets the guidelines for permanence and durability of the Commit-
tee on Production Guidelines for Book Longevity of the Council on Library Resources. ∞

For
Ellen, of course,
and for
George Garrett,
in loving memory

Contents

I

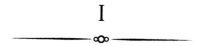

Old Age Begins

1.

Not with my grandfather in the mirror
or the mall clerk who thinks my search
for ink that comes in a bottle
means dementia, but with driving into
a B movie sunset toward Brigham
and Women's Hospital, the doctor
on my cellphone saying their procedure
is too risky for your condition. Old age begins
when you don't remember giving me
a wrenched smile and folding
into a phrase of gibberish on the beach,
where the dog went on crouching for a ball
I wouldn't be tossing—the odd image
registered as I punched in 911. It begins
as you're leaving the dunes with two EMTs
in the bed of a pickup, then tourists
around the ambulance, this free gawk
a part of their two-week package. Plugged
in to intensive care, "Why is this
being done to me?" As though you'd newly
gotten religion. Beside myself
at your bedside, watching myself
watching you, I'm a bystander in two lives.

2.

Now you must learn to write your name
as in first grade, but other-handed,
and not with a pen like a dybbuk's finger
and ink as if from a mudhole in the desk,
not with that rippy gray school paper
this time. If the rolls of practice cursive
recall barbed wire, this time
it's not that kind of war. You've come

tottering out of a stroke on a skinny cane,
not fast but accurate, learning to walk
again, vestigial babytalk in your
"Don't overload my washington machine,"
and "Pass me that cross hop bun." When you
were a little girl coming home down
the hill one day from school, an American
wind snatched you. Remember how you
cried out *Unten gesetzt mir!* until it
relented and set you down further along
the sidewalk? You must fight this
fight, too. You will not have to escape
over the Alps into Italy this time.

3.

As I was loading the feeder
so your favorite the red-bellied
woodpecker would be there
when you woke this morning,
I discovered that there was
a rhythm to all this.

I had already picked your pockets
of tissues and loaded the laundry
downstairs, then scraped
the breakfast clatter and loaded
the dishwasher, careful not to
rouse you with all that dissonance,

and tied paper knots but didn't let
the dog catch and test them
for tightness as usual before
I loaded them, topped off
with kindling and splits, into
the woodstove with barely a clank.

So many ampersands, so many loads,
so much onomatopoeia before
the active verbs: listening for
the right drone from the basement,
planning whole wheat bread
for the oven, hearing the dishwasher
groaning through its cycles.

After more than a year of this
I'm learning the pleasures of process
otherwise than on the page.
While I was aimed at poems
in another room, you had made poetry
of these household steps toward order,
which now in your illness I try,
neither in drudgery nor
for the piling up of chits in heaven.

4.

Just for tonight I promise not to call
the calamari you've ordered "squid,"
or remark how its consistency
is like those rubber bands
the post office bundles mail in.

We've come to Salty's
because the seafood's local
and we're local, because
we won't have to negotiate
the tourists downtown, and you
can get from the parking lot
to a table with your cane.

Forty years ago today
your maid of honor passed out

in the cornfield. I forget the name
of that guest who afterwards
(commanded, he claimed,
by William Blake) tried to walk
to Sunderland naked
to visit the woman he loved.

We must have blinked because
we are here alone but alive together.
The children, those grownups, are with
their children, or working on syllabi
they think embody their futures.

Just for tonight I won't say how
all those lozenges in the organizer
I call your buzzbox remind me
of SciFi movies. Wasn't Zocor
the evil doctor whose pointed ears
kept coming unglued, and Celexa
the space princess? Their planet
was Depakote, as I recall. This is
all too real for that,
like the Warfarin you take
against the warfare in your brain.

One small glass of wine won't make you dream
again about our police station attic,
which is generously stocked
with abandoned wheelchairs, canes,
braces and crutches, and looks
to you like a small-town Lourdes.

II

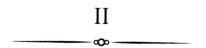

Walking Will Solve It

Or so the Romans prescribed.
A half-mile down the Egg Island flats
the fridge can't mumble
its imprecations at me, the bills, taxes
and toxins seem to be sloughing off,
all the home stuff that makes me feel
I'm a man up there on a steel span
over the river, painting each beam
with a small brush, doing it all alone.

Now I'm humming, recalling the lyrics
of old tunes I didn't know I knew. I think of
Stevens largely pontificating to himself
all the way down Farmington Avenue
to the office, then Wordsworth and Coleridge
on gravel and scrubby paths, Frost
out walking the dark. With two dogs
I never walk alone, for they have things
to show me. Lefty may pick up a squid
so recently dead it is still that purply
fresh squid color, or a green crab
will be waving its wrenches around
in Magnus's mandibles so I have to
talk him into dropping it.

Where tall spartina obscures
the marsh channels that drain and fill
with the tides, I have dreamed two men
walking on water for an instant, before their barge
rounded the bend and there were four, one poling,
one hanging onto the tiller, and two rowing,
seated in the bow before piled hay
and the haying machine. Ghosts of the Portuguese
farmers, and the dream boat for old age,
the Charon update. A windless, fetorless heat

like sepia filled the dream's air, and swimming
behind those oarsmen a huge head like a gray seal's—
the old horse whose name I'm somehow
certain is Joseph, out of harness, a halo of greenflies
and mosquitoes dissolving around his ears.

Back of the Egg Island dunes once,
a woman's footprints, toes flawless, mild arch,
heel slender, going side-by-side with a set of paws
whose arrowhead shape and flat heel
meant coyote. Too early for bare feet,
she was pushing the season. Then a blue heron's
tracks appeared beside hers, clean as
a Norse mapmaker's sign for forest. Girl with Heron,
Girl and Coyote, as in a myth like the Boy and
the Dolphin. They walked all the way to the tideline,
but if reason kicks in it will say she was following
the previous meanders as I was following hers,
that I could never wake early enough
to watch her re-enter the sea.

But this morning, stranded in a pool
the river deposited, a small fish flashing back and forth
as though one of those times that puddle
would lead to the river's freedom—
it brought me back to the man on the bridge,
who sooner or later has to begin again
where he started.

Links

Those zooplankton drifts—
bottom stocks in the great soup
of being—are aggregating now
in places around the bay. Undersea
clouds are thickening with krill
and larval swimmers, sea butterflies
and beings so small they could travel
in our blood. Radiolarians
like minute satellites are attracting
the spouts that blow images of trees
briefly over water, and even onshore
we catch the sunlit backs of right
whales slipping toward sustenance—
the Right Whale because oil-rich
and slow-going, a floater once
the harpoon found its heart.
A tenth of maybe three hundred
survivors are here now,
socializing and making their
plankton-filtering runs between
Long Point and the Manomet
Hills, on Stellwagen Bank,
and all the way from the Race
to the ocean off the Highland
clay pounds. They do not
recognize shipping lanes or
the concept of hull strike.
On a tanker's bridge, at the wheel
of the *Little Infant,* who sees
the single stunned-water print
that's left when a whale dives,
how it looks as if the surface
were beginning the change to ice?

You Were a Leaf Clump in the Cherry Tree

yellowing early, caught in the netting
I swaddled the branches with
to keep birds like you off. How long
had you hung there, hours, a day,
upside down and silent as though
you'd given up? I must have passed
several times without seeing,
and finally, *Dead* I thought,
a young or female orchard oriole,
but a lift of the netting started
your squalls, keeping you at it
and at the fingers of my work gloves,
your efficient bugsticker
even clamping the scissors
as I took you off the tree, wrapped
in a reticule of net. It was almost
surgical, the way I worked
around the breast, and the tense feet
gripping strands, the closest
in years I've come to that dogfish
and cat I dissected in labs
when I intended to cure cancer.
Between panics you seemed
to understand I was freeing you,
trying to do no harm, snipping away
the layers that involved you, trying
to unbind those wings, your crucial
difference, but you dropped too soon
free-footed to the deck and under,
unreachable with a grandchild's
plastic shovel, another good intention
gone quiet again and out of sight
as others you couldn't join
flashed pumpkin and black, passing
through the afternoon for the south.

Postcard

For a hundred feet across the sand,
a smooth path dragged along the edge
of eelgrass in the wintry
dunes behind Egg Island, the way
a gardener might haul a sack of kelp home.

But then the runic prints of a great blue heron
alongside, proof of the culprit, and where
the dragging ended the hand,
black, glovelike, human
almost with its gray individual nails.

Not claws, not reptilian, but mammalian
nails, a development beyond flipper
and fin. Then the attached skeletal armature,
a limb picked clean from its brief radius
and ulna to the scapula's finality.

I will not write *Wish you were here with your*
sunblock and umbrella. The winter beach
is not the summer beach. It was a seal, I'd guess,
strayed too far from the salt refuge
to wherever the pack trapped her.

Useless to wonder where,
her parts divvied up and distributed among
the pillagers and scrounges of the earth
and air, who know when you're near
and are gone.

This Morning's Pep Talk at Egg Island

Even the kids negotiating friendships
on that yellow schoolbus racketing past
know it's a different scenario
every day, not just the same elemental
hostilities like ocean versus sand,
tough places to make a living.
                              To see things
as they are, keep your eyes open. This morning
on the bay side of Egg Island I watched
as water instantly grew a head—a gray seal
arriving for winter, no being more seamlessly
suited to its métier.
                        Wings alternating black
and white will be another grand opening
if you lift your own head out of theory
in time to catch the orange-brown flash
and shift of snow buntings.
                           Knock those quotes
off "reality" and work with it. Yesterday
I had to set a blue-headed vireo
hitting a window against the way a merlin
running down a flicker screaming
just above my head—I felt both wingdrafts
passing—lost her this time in the trees.

Nothing like a little gift here
and there to help nudge things your way:
consider the nuthatches talking together
where suet's hung in the striped
maple's golden canopy.

                        Calculate, cultivate
the proximity of happenings to happiness,

and take your disappointments by the throat,
the way that praying mantis who cringed
childlike at the introduction of my stick
into her world grabbed it with both hands
the second time, manipulating it
to let me know how strong she was.

Ghost Gear

All that we know of it for sure
are these washed-up knots
of miracle fiber, citrus-colored
tangles the sea cannot rot
but over time will chew
and abrade with patience
to filaments, and these plank ends
whose bolts have rusted
to bond with wood.

Only these fractions of the sea's
divisions, though they
hint at things waiting. Not
a tentacled Jules Verne
chimera raving down there,
but things accreting
to themselves bivalves, weed, mud.

A bashed lobster pot as threatening
onshore as a broken baby stroller,
cutaway nets you might see
on the ceiling at the Clam Shack—
but to anyone who puts down
a trawl or a dredge
out there, potent as a steel
snarl of wire to snag—even
flip—a hull: ghost gear,
first of a trinity with
Mayday and widowmaker.

Adding It Up

The name's *Time Bandit* on the transom
of a trawler whose beam is too wide
for the lane. Getting down Route 28
behind it will take a while, but at least

the diesel blasts off the cab
and the shimmy of seaweed
like hula skirts on either
side of the hull are distractions.

What you hear this time of year
at the bar or next booth at the diner
is, "I'm a sixty-year-old captain
with an eighty-year-old hull."

Cod's high in the market, low on the docks,
and the mackerel have vanished.
Midwater trawlers suck the catch up
like an Electrolux.

Today the harbor's a gray heave,
the dunes so lapped with snow
the Arctic comes to mind. No crewman
would admit that Stellwagen Bank

puts something in the red corpuscles
when the moon rises and the only
life in the world is on that deck.

The *Time Bandit*'s got civil serpents
boxing it in with permit banks and mesh sizes.
Seals and dogfish follow in its wake. Still,
it's on its way to the boatyard for
another overhaul.

Fish here not there, yesterday
but not next week. The crew's got leased
and traded quotas, catch shares, more like
brokers than fishermen. Remembering
how bread-and-butter nets could draw

a half ton of yellowtail with one pass,
no At-Sea Monitor on board to throw a fish-fit
over the by-catch, they're doing the math,
too old to stay in, too broke to get out.

Wild Guesses

Who do they think we are? It wasn't
the young coyote on the road,
leggy, recently out of the den
and innocent of cars
that prompted the question, nor
even a pair of willets near their nest
behind Egg Island, unwitting
about how their wings'
distraction display evokes
a history of gunners
who'd never touch them
with a knife and fork.

That cecropian flight I thought
a luna moth's one morning
in the kitchen never set off
the questioning either, although
trapped between screen
and sliding door it proved
a thing like crepe
and safety pins: a bat.

It took a crab bald as a baby
to start it, stranded by
low tide and studying me—
What am I? It could never have seen
anything like me upright
on the sea's floor. An unchildlike
glow of assessment
lit those eyes as it raised
the whole carapace of its head,
even turned to follow my going
as I left it to itself and the sun
and whatever water
might return in a few hours.

The Evidence of Four March Mornings

Deliverer and undertaker, a full moon tide
dropped the harbor seal on the flats,
already thick with gasses. Its back flippers,
almost feet, politely enfolded each other,
or so it appeared from the distance the dog
and I kept. Already from one end
on the second morning a red gut pile
was extruded. It was like a battlefield corner
awaiting ravens, though just one gull,
one of the sea's janitors, strode
the remaining silver skin, working.

Entrails had been dragged around by
day three, and the ribs were a ruddy basket.
The skull was eye sockets and a mouth
that recalled Munch's *The Scream*. A fox
walked out of the dunes and around the scene,
a study in nonchalance, a foreman
looking for the best approach, but returned
the way it had come, as though
the distant dog and I squelched hunger.

Two black-backed gulls in a squawk
on the fourth morning, a quandary
over the space between them, in which was
nothing, not even a brief reticulation
in red, all evidence erased, as though the sea
had had enough barbarity, or was sick of
life lessons, or knew another sandspit
where its working poor needed
whatever sustenance remained.

Ars Poetica: The Foxes

What will make it red as that one
years ago by the woodpile, a fox that loitered
as though in revelation's flames for
a telltale whiff of rodent beneath the snow?
Not these windfall apples hard as cueballs
in the cold, not even that pumpkin I recycled
to its plot as too big and stringy for a pie,
folded now into a white turban. Snow
is on the ground this January dusk,
and this fox, flat black and gray,
no burning bush, walks without hurry
among the fruit trees, then behind the shed
and is gone. Barely a fox at all, barely more
than a tremor of wind in the bushes
behind the orchard, it needs a tidbit
of cottontail or field mouse, the under-shed
holdouts against January, small
and blooded, to stagger its foxprints
too fastidiously placed.

Night Flight

A fuzzy burr above my head, you woke me,
escaped I thought from the dream place
into this February night, the moonlight
ringing outside like iron on the snow.
Then you were buzzing around my skull,
maybe sensing brainfold heat escaping
through the faults a truck gave me
when I was nine and dashing for home
after Tommy Hendry's mother caught us
lowering her son two stories
in a rope and crate arrangement.

You're months early, and must have
thawed out of the stovewood I brought in
yesterday. But who are you, puzzling
yourself in the dark about me, struggling
through my forearm's undergrowth?
Not a junebug strumming as though
its bald music is a ticket to the light,
but one of those other summer screen lives
that seem impromptu, assembled for
one evening, put together of whatever
detritus is lying around—
bits of cornshock, seedcoat, petal, twig.

Are there eyespots on your wings that
make you look like the local anchorwoman,
or red eyes blinking in the dark
so you seem an escapee from a gospel's
illuminated margin? No matter.
Be a cranial effusion or winged crustacean
soul hatched from a glaucous web

down in the cauldron of the marsh, be one
of whatever this dark makes possible,
a welcome traveler of the synapses
between leaps of being.

Midden

My shovel rang against this pile
in January, this midden and menu
of a lost year. No promises there.
It was a rock of snow, weather's
depository, not dirt at all, but came

true again in the March rains,
a supermuck raccoons visited
with articulate digits, and skunks
nosed as though some tramp was
poking around with his walking stick.

The ocean warming above fifty now,
the last frost a week ago
melted off the shed roof, I open this
kitchen history to feed
forthcoming shoots and sprawls,

drive my shovel into the wormworks
we lubricated with each morning's
coffee grounds, out-takes from our table,
shuckings, stones and pits, a furred
mango seed the size of a wallet, all of it

seasoned with buckets of stove ash, the dust
of a winter's oak and maple, kibble
gone green, squashrot and apple ferment—
remembering even the planet's
a collection of cosmic leftovers.

Already mussel shells empurpled
by the weather have donated calcium,

and this crustacean armor has softened
and given its reds to the heat
that breaks everything down.

Soon this mound will attract
a platoon of crows to arrange sentries
and scouts in the pines
before the fly-in, their wing music
one more pleasure of the morning.

Seed Packet

In three months' time it will seem
as though you bought
a 99-cent ticket to the Big Top:
a small green vehicle with orange
circus hubcaps will appear
in your garden, and send out of
every exit pattypans
yellow and green, clearing your fence
in their ruffs
and frills, and still more
clowns of the vegetable kingdom
will brave thistles in striped, edible hats
dangled with a marigold
here and there for keeping bugs away,
the whole troupe freckled
variously and sniffing the daylilies
with zucchini beezers and golden honkers,
not a nose in sight, but impossible blue
hubbard shoes fleeing up the paths
on their lifelines.

Elegy for a Border Collie

1.

As though they'd turned you into a cake
or an Easter bonnet, the box they handed me
was white, with a silver ribbon, and heavier
than it looked, and lit a red
scribble of rage in the air before my eyes.

I wanted to set it on the counter and begin
dismantling the vet's office one stick at a time,
then go for the shrubbery outside,
yelling "I want my dog back," like a child
who doesn't know the rules.

Remembering that last day how you hung
your head expecting punishment
though you'd done nothing wrong, and your eyes
saying you knew, and all the way home
from New Hampshire, fifteen years ago . . .

But I settled for a verbal shot: "Looks like a goddam
birthday present." And the girl, "You didn't want
an urn, remember?" Another damp-eyed
functionary, Finnbarr. The ones she'd shown me
looked like bowling trophies.

I could have told her they'd go broke if people
really let their grief hang out, trying to carry
the ashes home in burlap sacks
and scrapwood coffins that looked like kids'
defective soapbox cars.

2.

Before the tides at winter solstice
gathered the last of you in, the end of your confusions
and random terrors was a glitter of bone chips
in a meager line of ashes on the flats
where you loved to retrieve a ball.

Until the air—tearing in a rush above me there
one January morning—became a flock, white
when it flashed together on a turn, heading for the river,
hundreds flattening over the surface, wings scissoring,
way late in the year for a migration,

and balling into unity again, a gathering of least
sandpipers, wowing like fireworks now
over Egg Island, particles driven by a power
beyond them, maybe building their resolve
before crossing the next southward Atlantic reach.

Between them and you, old dog, I found myself
standing among so much I do not know
about matter's translations and the shifts of being
that I gave myself up to what I saw.

Names by a River

The keels of the *Speedwell* and *Discoverer*
four hundred years ago passed over
where I am walking among the glasswort
and hudsonia this morning, the river's
estuary here then. Before Bradford
and Miles Standish you came
with fifty men in armor out of Bristol,
barely a man yourself, nevertheless
Captain Martin Pring, from your portrait
I'd say a handy little dude like Standish
and John Smith, your chin-beard sharp
as a poinado. Enough mitten-shaped leaves
of the sassafras here to make a homeward cargo
for both holds, you calculated—a possible cure
for the French pox. A kingbird works
the dune grasses for insects this morning,
at what you named Whitson Bay after
a prime investor in your voyage.

All that is left of 1603 has been shifted,
wind and sea, ground down, sorted, re-pummeled,
blown sideways, sea and wind, processed and
overlain with grasses and snows among the vagaries
of the river, itself renamed: Pamet now for the tribe
you pressed into flight with the mastiffs
Gallant and Fool. After a few thousand walks
among the nesters here, I call these dunes
and flats Egg Island, in part to confuse
the local hiking club, identical in their
baggy shorts and yellow t-shirts, their catalog
explorer hats, outfits absurd as those you gifted
the natives with, those "divers sorts of
meanest merchandise."

Who do I think I am, since only change
is unchanging here: Whitson's Bay
to Egg Island, and your Mount Aldworth
to Tom's Hill, after a last Pamet
who lived up there? Even the French pox
has run through a litany of names,
not many as impugning, but all as colorful,
the Grandgore, the Black Lion,
and the sassafras itself went into
root beer. You stayed seven weeks, then sailed
from the August heat inimical to northern blood.

Since mariners read the birds, though
you wouldn't have names for some, no doubt
you saw the flocks dropping down
and reforming for the south, semipalmated
plovers this morning, big name for a brief
flash of white with half-webbed feet,
their migration begun, but you didn't
stay on for the grand transitions—
a stray albatross, wing-broken, rolled over
the dunes in a January blow, or the way
a north wind surprises a walker as he faces
about into it. Pilgrims, briefly, converting
to whalers, then trap fishermen—would you
have called them *Portingales*?—
and the fish houses, ice houses, coal-fired freights,
and the river forever trying new entries and
departures between Corn Hill and Fisher's Beach,
scouring its bed into sandbars, undermining,
making runs up the valley, trying to join
the Atlantic at the farther shore.

And here, as I read the flats this morning,
going side-by-side with a set of tracks, a dog
at first, but no mastiff: feet too narrow,
heel pads flat at the back, and no splay,
so more likely a coyote, perhaps one of those
you called "dogs with sharp and long noses."
The names never stick, as if in the naming
the thing itself is changed. These whorls
in the riverbed could be the fingerprint of God,
and the slow motion whip-cracks of the river
keep flexing over time between headlands.

III

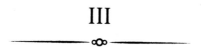

I Am the Donkey of Blind Raftery

I lugged panniers of turf and scutched corn,
hay on the hay-bogy, manure in a tip-cart,
seaweed for mulching, practical loads all,
but now this tramp poet sings
in a failing tongue at my shoulder,
leaning across me toward every
ignorant ear on the roads of Galway.

Who were you expecting, Pegasus?
A Connemara pony? That's fodder for those
ferocious aunties the schoolmasters.
My name is Poteen Jack, and just because
my story circles about a star

halted above a stable where ragged faces
breathed their warmth upon a god,
they pass a child seven times
over and under me, red string around
her throat to cure the chin cough.

I am not all peace and patience
under this roughage, so get
your eyeful of the two of us,
then get the hell out of our way.

Look at this stumbler Raftery,
who never falters when he sings his vision
of Mary Hynes—though she'll die ancient
with mumbling under leaky thatch
at the back of a bog, recalling her ruin
at the hands of a big-house sportsman.

Look at Raftery, who lost the dark in his eyes
one night when Death clacked through
his room in an ivory rig-up, but had
his blindness back by morning.

And look at me, shaggy and mean-mouthed
enough to support poetry, picking my way
and his through a mockery of magpies,
up boreens and down the ditchbacks
from Loughrea to Ardrahan,
my only wage his next song in my ear.

The Donegal People

1.

That morning on a Rathmullan pier,
blood was calling to blood across Lough Swilly—
They came from someplace over there.
I wandered around Inishowen graveyards
on the far side of *Sliabh Sneachta,*
the Snowy Mountain, but no old man appeared
like a figure out of folklore to weave
the fabric whole, telling
who the first was to watch the Inishtrahull
lighthouse sinking astern of a vessel
pointed for America, the first to wear shoes
every day of the week, and which Bridget
witnessed the marriage of this Timothy
or another to that Mary Margaret,
and who Tailor Barr and Brains Edward were.

Nobody connected the Boston suburbs
with Clonmany, Isle of Doagh, Ballyliffin,
Ballyloskey and Cabadooey for me,
places on the farther slopes
of that snowy mountain. At times
it was only the memory of a name, Aunt Celia,
Aunt Lizzie; once an elegant ankle
disappearing into a Buick after a funeral,
and that was Cousin Marion. But where,
in what slot, to fit Little Danny McElenny,
insurance agent and bookmaker?

Which Brian was last seen near
the fishpiers along Atlantic Avenue? A troll
rips into the parish records and someone's gone
into the air. Someone sails for Scotland
to harvest potatoes and never comes home.

A daughter is called Denny's Annie's Rosie.
A daughter is named for her sister
taken with diphtheria.

Fires, wars, poteen, a village buried under
a sandstorm one night in an old century. All those
March 17th birthdays on census rolls were
a way of backhanding authority,
and those birth years inventions of a folk
who had tentative relations with calendars
and the facts. Forget the timeline. Follow
Salty Jack to Trinity, Newfoundland,
and the boys from Carndonagh
down the mineshafts at Butte, Montana.

Follow Imelda and Con into various
Irish Bayous and Hungry Hills. So as not to be
worked to death, who put immigration
in reverse and went home to Malin Head?
Why did the little grandchildren think
the old people had a language of their own?

2.

St. Joseph's Parish, Roxbury

We dead slip out of memory in stages:
acidic Boston soil, this burial ground
identified beside the church in the 1884
city atlas, gone in the next edition
six years later. We Famine immigrants
who rose from the steerage of
coffin ships to raise St. Joseph's church
have served more than a century
in this purgatory of bones, anonymous,

our only stone a broken tablet reading,
Donegal, Ireland. I remember the crowing
of other sets of bones about to be moved
because their families got a leg up,
the lace-curtain, two-toilet Irish, soon
to be replanted under celtic crosses
in new cemeteries the diocese opened:
"Sure, they tend them places like
putting greens." After the roof fell in,
St. Joe's might have been mistaken
for any stranded west country ruin
Cromwell had torched and the rain blowing
off the Atlantic had rotted. All it lacked
was the cropping sheep. Somehow
over the century, four feet of topsoil arrived
and grew grass. Call it site improvement.
Two maples grew, generous enough
to sign treaties under. And the rumors grew:
unmarked graves, the poor who are always
with us. To facilitate Sunday parking,
one side of our field was black-topped.
An army of curates and monsignors, lying
or in denial or too lazy to check
until the real estate legalities forced it—
our field's to go for a new high school—
found a few bones that had strayed.
Above us the scratching and brushing
has started in, no louder than mouse work.
I'd scream it if I could: this isn't archaeology,
it's buried shame. These bones are an education
for the new schoolkids about what a life
is worth. I might as well have starved
on a slope of *Sliabh Sneachta,*
a handful of boiled nettles in my mouth.

Sidetracking

Because you don't trust me on Irish roads
whose ditches are visited by magpies,
their iridescences and drawn-out tails
tending to distract me from driving on the left,
you got behind the wheel as we set out
for Malin Head, the top of Donegal,
where they claimed we might see the distillery
smokestacks on Islay, across the water
in the Hebrides. Was it the miles
behind that woman barely herding a roadwide
trot of sheep on her motorbike that put us
off our route before she turned them out
into a field near Umgall? Or was it that—
caught between the hearse and rental buses
in a village funeral—we were forced to stay on
for the obsequies, eye-catching among suspicious
mourners, until a man who'd maybe never been
where we were going could put us right?
Eleven weathers in an hour and we were lost
in cloud-creep fluctuating between
salmon and crowberry, the sea and the flow
of landscapes, boulders with peach striations
beside a thread of road among fields and hills
whose names on the ordnance map
sounded like the smashing of crockery.
Until, above us in midflight, one more
reminder that in Ireland any map
is approximate, only its gifts of sidetracking
guaranteed. *Coour-lee.* As if a girl's name
were turning into music, and I saw
as you drove how well a curlew can sail
with its beak that looks as out-of-symmetry
as those antlers they say
dragged the Irish elk into extinction.

On the Sea of the Hebrides

Struth nam Fear Gorm

Off Sollay with Davy MacNeil one evening,
hauling creels among the seabirds reveling
in the long summer light, I stretched
to ease a knot from my spine, and saw
on the edge of vision off there,
its dark bulk somewhere between charcoal
and juniper, an island, its mountain
indigo, where the North Atlantic
should be open all the way to Canada.

Unsteady with surprise—wave tremor
under the hull, or a sudden shift
of the Hebridean light?—I looked back
at the defiled gannet and fulmar tenements,
solid on the rock face of the Sgurr.
Cries of the guillemots and razorbills had ceased,
and seaward, the shadow of a cloud moved
across that island's slopes, now cornflower blue
above peat-colored foreland.

"Davy?" I said, and pointed. He shook a reluctant
lobster from a creel into the holding tank.
"That's Fulva," he said, matter-of-fact: "It turns up
off there every little while. It can't be reached
anymore, that island, and you can't ever predict it.
If it's not to the south of here it's to the north.

"They said it was down around Mulliskay
a week or two ago. In the goneby, people
would go out to it to speak the old tongue
with them that lives there, but we lost the way to it

41

when we lost that way of speaking. They say
it's a place where a change would be no improvement.
Back a year or three ago, a boatload from the Center
for Numinous Phenomena sailed for it, bristling
like a hedgehog with antennas, and reached close enough
to see that there was people lounging about
the quay in the evening. But that island has less
substance now than mist on a leaf, and the boat went
right through it, so they say."

Pennies: A History

Raking a generation of oak leaves
out of my mother's flowerbeds,
salamander habitat,
as she used to excuse it,
we turned the dull pennies up
among brown, empty
Old Thompson pints, and checked
each coin for a worthwhile Indian head.

How much was it about copper
for her roses, a tip she had garnered
from "The Weekend Cultivator,"
and how much was Inishowen custom,
a way of buying
the patronage of earthly powers?

The whiskey I could explain
simply by naming Tom Bray's carpenters,
those constant smilers who worked on the house
the summer I was eight: Bassett and Woods;
Ryder, on his good days;
Froggy, in those first cowboy boots
I'd laid eyes on outside the silver screen.

Next year I'd collect the two-cent
deposits on Nemasket Cola bottles
that hot-toppers and truckers
tossed on the grass when they widened
the state road, good as cash for grape soda
and orange at Mr. Davis's store. Then
it was hearing a B&M fish freight
a half mile off in the pineys,
the secret between it and me
a few pennies laid on the tracks.

But how many of my mother's
were really about being able
to throw them away? Like eating
potatoes without their jackets,
another way of saying, *The Famine
is over, and we are survived.* A habit
learned from her mother, Mary Barr,
who arrived here from Carndonagh
clutching pennies of her own, as though
they were the keys to a new world.

Some Fragments of Senan the Anchorite

1.

Boat-knock across open water
wakes him up, wood-hollow thudding
of oars against thole pin and gunnel,
and he rises with care from stone
pillow and slab, popping a shoulder
into place, kicking out to crack a knee
back into working order, as though
on his durable bed, fog-drizzled,
all night under his skin his bones
had wandered with his dreams.

Square-sailed offshore, brim full
and more with singing boys, a great
tub's wallowing along, going
he knows where upriver. *Stranger,*
the steersman shouts, *is this the way*
to Clonmacnoise?

No other, he croaks back. *From which*
far country has the name and repute of Ciaran
drawn such impeccant faces today?

And the mariner calls, *Jibjabber, Barleyview,*
Vasseroy, maybe Stole-a-goose. Take
your choice, they are all one to me. These
I took aboard at Galway. They are grogged up
on holy fire. It makes them smile, and sing
like an Iberian trader's parrot cage.

Clonmacnoise will water that fire
and break those smiles like twigs,
Senan says. *A year or two of being*
copyboys and they'll be diddling

in the margins over golden hair
and berry-tasting lips they dream about
but wouldn't touch when they were
near at hand. I've seen it all before
at Skellig Michael. As for disciples,
better a school of bream
than those gulled boys.

That boat was out of
hearing now, soon out of sight.
There drifted down to Senan
from upriver either a distant cantlet
of their singing, or inarticulate wind.

2.

From Sinainn, woman of the source,
there drifted downstream to Senan
salmon in plenty,
                  spear-food he took
in the shallows, each pink filet
a slab of knowledge in the flesh.

Somewhere in the Land of Promise
up there, the Spring of Segais
rises from her silver cauldron,
he believes,
               and nine hazel trees
lean over to drop their nuts
and nourish these fish,
                    which is why
their flesh in his sends him
going and doing, raises him up
mornings in health.
                Two eggs
of the redthroat who flies bearing

a heavy head on its narrow neck
he sent her in return,
                              fawn brown
and darker spotted, still in their moss
in a basket woven of holly he set
on the water.
                    Teal who wear
the quarter moon on their cheeks
the smith must have hammered
into her cauldron,
                      and grebes
who sail their babies along on
their backs,
                    and the curlew,
whose intelligence is in
the curved beak that leads him
the right direction,
                          these too
she poured from her cauldron
into the river for him, their breast meat
hearty and dark.
                      Therefore, of the tree
whose juices distill
to a honey that lights the brain
with the power of wine,
                            he sent her
a crock wrapped in grasses,
recumbent in a cradle of holly.

3.

Flann the poet was a joiner
and a schemer. Dipping a blade
in any pot he could bull a shoulder
through to reach, ever on lookout
for a cartful of his fellows and

47

a hand up. So ambitious I have
seen him drool from both corners
of his mouth at once, and sweat
a wine-slick over position
and preferment. You can hear
in his verses the little chieftain
waving a dull spear to draw
attendance to him, and the rhythms
of Fionn of Glasheen, albeit
stumbling, and the textures of
Aenghus Mor, albeit lisped.
But that is the way of tufthunters
who come to that trade early
and are given lunulae and rings
in the great halls, heelers with
only wit enough to kneel,
who cannot stand up straight
in their own lines unless some
doddering clientage lifts them.
Yearly thereafter Flann was
given tributes, public encomia
at Tara and elsewhere, his name
common as profanity on the lips
of his boys, *Flann this, Flann that,*
until, a wallow of puffery, a swan
of self-regard, a prowhead trailing
a wake of lickspittle, dispensing
significance as sensible as
his blurbs, a hen feathered in
envy, his tongue thick as a bullock's
yet sharp as swordgrass against
all comers, and still unable to sort
an oystercatcher from a stonechat,
he pricked himself on the point
of his own avarice and folded

to a heap of dewlaps. Necropolized
up there at Terryglass, his toadies
traipsing off with his successor,
no boy will try on any slender girl
a line of his, no mother's
lullabies will be his songs.

IV

Sprezzatura

A few men in Milton, West Virginia,
have it. They go to work in cut-off jeans,
tee shirts and sneakers, casual as
going to the park for a softball game.
Each begins his day by dipping
a hollow steel rod into molten glass
the color of egg yolk, and twirling it
to hold the roundness, keeping the form,
making it look easy as stirring
your coffee, though it must be more like
spinning a swirl of the sun. Then back
and forth to the furnace's glory hole,
2100 Fahrenheit, lest it cool and crack,
knowing gravity wants it, and just
how much breath to send through the rod
and how fast, lest it wobble into
a cartoon bubble, as lopsided with hot air
as a politico's promises, and crash
to common glass on the floor. *Sprezzatura,*
a High Renaissance word for the skill
and recklessness that releases grace,
a seemingly offhand act that conceals
the pains taken. This gaffer seated
like the chief alchemist has it,
and accepts in silence that rod
and molten ball—blue now, from a turn
in a serious vat—rolling it, concentrating,
a touch and a tweak with tools dipped
in water. A nod here and there, but nobody
has said a word. This long-necked
exclamation appears to be their gloss
on the nonchalance of those
who play with fire.

An Evel Knievel Elegy

We have all felt our parachutes
malfunctioning at a job interview
or cocktail party, with bystanders
reading the freefall on our faces,
and some of us have imagined
how it must have felt for you
above the Snake River Canyon
or the fountains outside Caesars
Palace, though a mental bungee
reversed our flops before we were
converted to sacks of poker chips and spent
a month or more in a coma. You were
our star-spangled Icarus, Evel,
while we dressed off the rack
for working lives among the common
asps and vipers, never jumping
the rattlers in what you and
the networks considered a sport.
Stunts, Evel. We loved their heights
and distances from our gray quotidian
so much we bought the kids three
hundred million dollars' worth
of your wheels and get-ups. You were
our airborne Elvis, and rode
your rocket-powered bike through fire.
Which we admired, though some,
annealing or annulled, knew that
they stand in fire all their lives,
and turned away, and didn't applaud,
and would not suffer the loss
of your departure.

The Day After

1.

November first, for instance, with the Dead
rained upon but still upright on the lawn
around the bandstand, urban scarecrows
gaping through their mascara jags as though
in awe of the wind herding leafage so the sky
can present its own *memento mori.*

Where's that big-haired one who
jump-started me yesterday by raising
a camera among these orthodontists'
nightmares formalized in black?
That robot or photographer prompted
questions about the Quick and the Dead,
Samhain of the Celts and the wall
let down between worlds,
sooner restored if you drive on
into the workaday of the day after.

2.

Or take St. Stephen's Day, December 26, a green
trashbag fitted back over the artificial tree,
peak star and tinsel, toy sleds, bulbs and all,
then down the basement stairs. *Men,*
my daughter exasperates. Meaning,
No sense of ritual, no advent before
the event, and no recessional.

Time enough for closure, but not to summon
the images of Santas past, that one carried out
as if by pallbearers—the children appalled—

after a night of yuletide cadging, and that other
in the mall parking lot, waving a cellphone
and growling through a faceful of white strings,
"Beat it, punks. I'll call the cops."

Carolina Déjà Vu

When my daughter's pit bull Lilith
began dragging me toward a line of cedars
bordering the field, I gripped her leash
in both hands and leaned back
as though water-skiing, letting
her take all my weight more slowly
across those dips and swells of grass

toward whatever back there
was moving fast and keeping to
the trees, buffeting branches,
haunch of a big dog I thought I saw,
or a jogger, until a black bear
went galloping down the tree line.

Suddenly oxygen-deprived, I saw things
as through thick glass in the August heat
that had dropped its deep-sea diver's
helmet over me and was starting
to knot the source of air.

Then the sirens, adding their wail
to the cicadas, taking the curse off
the fireplug dog yapping and leaping
as if to offer us up as prime morsels,
her purple tongue flagging,

and taking me back fifty years
to the kind of misery that made
our mother wring her hands—My boys
are so wild! Even a bear foraging
among the motels and gas stations
at the city's edge might approximate

human misery at seven o'clock
on a Sunday morning—a quart of
maple walnut or a bag of chips
at the Zipmart, say—and
a solid citizen out walking a dog

might root for the bear as it drove
to a chainlink fence it never even
paused to puzzle out, but took it
as a teen-aged felon would,
one crash in the yaupon
and crape myrtle and gone.

The Black Humvee and the Blue Tangs

I FEAR O
—Humvee license plate

Driver, I too fear nothing, or should I say
reverting to nothing, or King Lear's
nothing, which may be as obscure to you
as the nothing that is not there
and the nothing that is. Caught up to you
near the harbor, all black and chrome
like the logo for something
that might be called the New Puritanism;

at least you're taking your time, so I can
absorb your message instead of studying
those anchored widowmakers the ice
is locking into Snow's Cove. Or is it that
you fear zero as citrus growers do? Zero
in school or even in the wallet, since
your vehicle gets ten miles to the gallon?

Is it Olive or Ophelia—an ex-wife
wild after more alimony? Passing the aquarium,
I recall the blue tangs or surgeonfish in their tank,
flat and ovoid, moving with elegance
in congregations, changing colors anywhere
between morning sky and a purple
that makes them seem as though
their own twilight accompanies them.

When attacked they project bony scalpels
from either side of the tail, and swim
alongside the offender swinging themselves.
I will not pass you to see if your eyes like theirs
look beyond alertness into woe, perhaps the result
of concealed weaponry. Their flesh is poisonous.

Plywood

Harry Cowell, 1913–1998

Wind pouring up the shore roads
sent a wild yelp hurtling the rooftree,

waking me so I thought you'd returned
on your hybrid bike, part Schwinn,

part swapshop, as when you'd stop
on the white line in the midst

of our empty pine-scape and howl
at the moon. Your way of celebrating

your own sheer animal spirits, I'd tell
anyone you frightened because

you scraped by on seafood, caught
or raked off the flats,

and the odd painting sold to a buyer
your sharpest eye had cleared.

*Not much we can afford to be
particular about, but my stuff's the world*

to me, and if I don't protect it, who will?
You renounced everything the rest of us

sweated for, so you'd chuckle when they
clucked that art had left you in shirtsleeves.

Who else could love the textures of plywood
secondhand, knots and the splintered

holes where nails got clawed out,
the irregular and jagged? Buffalo Sweeney

at the dump put them aside for you
to paint the tides on, water's motions

over the wood's stability, spontaneous
moves around the flaws—a dent where

a hammer missed a nailhead, the problem
of layers exposed, as on a cutbank.

S-curves, spirals, circles, zigzags
and you could render seas

and flung spray, light scattered
among a thousand strokes,

crashing blue, green, yes, but touched with
red, brown, grays up close. Bird's eye

was your appropriate slant, Harry,
or fisheye, as though the viewer sculled

along the air, self-contained as a kittiwake,
or could dive and stay under. You'd wave

a hand, dismiss the lack of human figures.
Look at old Claude Monet, it never hurt

his flowers. This one works to right about here.
You'd take the offending side off with a hacksaw.

Moonscape with Zipmart and Heron

Next morning, in one of the many Greenvilles
there are, its stripmall boulevards going
all night with kid cars chirping rubber,
he repacked his own car in the motel lot,
just as a blue heron, flying north,
drew its vestigial silence across the air,
giving shape and a sign to the morning
above the orange Zipmart that was still lit
like some techno-colony on the dry Mare Imbrium.
He did not think, *Desire without a You is only*
residue writ sideways. Or: *The Body is eternity's*
way of pushing our envelopes. He was gassed up,
but not that gassed up. Heading north,
he saw a line was there above those boulevards,
the demarcation of two cloud banks, but as though
mapping that great blue's passage: a hint,
he believed, of the tenacity in passing gristle
and bone, being somewhat bone and gristle himself,
and not of the dust inherent in orange cement-block bunkers.

Mayhem

It might be a skirt girls wear
for Beltane or another pastoral
occasion, in Eastern Europe
perhaps. You might see them
whirling in a painting by
one of the Generalic brothers,
maybe, "Spring Festival at
Hlebine," floralia we couldn't
name gracing the air about
their ankles. That morning
a mother probably announced,
"Today you can wear your
Mayhems to the dancing."
But this afternoon a redtail
flashed across my windshield
and landed, wings spread,
in the roadside grass, then
rose into the left lane
and flapped for five seconds
parallel to my car
before turning for the trees,
a limp attitude of surrender
dangling from its hook,
a spinal cord already snipped.
Behind glass it was as soundless
as a pantomime, but the mayhem
had already begun.

V

Striped Maple History

The stump looked like a medical illustration
of a heart, and its few wispy sprouts
showed me it wanted to live, so I planted it
by the door thirty years ago.

Each fall before the winds I still cut one side away
from the windows and trim out several fine
straight sticks sturdy enough for beanpoles.

So now, lopsided, a few branches looped and snaking,
it is grandly disreputable, nothing of the nursery
about it, and its three-lobed leaves, looking like
goose prints, turn yellow as October cools so it seems

fall's counterpoint to forsythia. Called goosefoot
some places, here it is nicknamed whistlewood:
a smart kid with a jackknife can reverse it to wood whistle.

Considered a pest of the understory by foresters,
it can live to be a hundred. I have stood under it
as a two-foot baby redtail hawk grappled through its twists,
wings trapped open or akimbo, shaking down

flocks of propellering fruit upon a fleeing chipmunk
and me. And all this spring a male yellowthroat
—a warbler with a black mask like a cartoon
housebreaker's—has been jerking its tail

as furiously as a wren and knocking at its own
reflection in the windows, defending its nest secreted
somewhere in the maple, even while showing

without knowing it that we have to look into
ourselves to look out for ourselves, and see
through our dubious aspects.

Smoke

1.

Red-legged with that streak of New Brunswick
wolf in its genes, pelt billowy in the wind,
the coyote I call Smoke stood right there

at my scrapwood pile yesterday morning,
maybe sniffing around for chipmunks
and field mice bunked in among my kindling.

Was it thirty years ago that first tall howl
lifted out of the marshgrass down there
and changed the content of our dusks?

The ropy scats dropped strategically on paths
came later, then a gray tail sticking
from a bush, too grand for squirrel.

2.

For their coloring and how they seem to appear
and vanish at will, I have called every one Smoke
since I saw what looked like a German shepherd

at sunrise overleaping a ten-foot thicket
of huckleberries no dog I know could jump,
a night rambler headed home, picking its way

across snowflats to drop without hesitation
out of sight, revealing the den that releases
the outcry of earache whenever a siren
passes on the highway, night or day.

3.

Against winter dunes, the stone-ax skull and arched
spine of a sick or trapped seal, all that remained,
with coyote prints advertising the feast. And as if
to deny the "lost cat" posters on phone poles,

in August Smoke lying out in the dunes
at binocular distance, sunning, maybe baking
its bones for what's coming, having already
detected a touch of it out of the North.

Last night in snow on the deck, clear
sets of prints, close, then closer,
under the hanging suet. As though

while I read fifteen feet away on the far side
of the glass, something was studying
the problem, like Aesop's fox those grapes.

Flute

Tapper and tinkerer, whenever
back in the trees a bird seemed
to be singing, *See see me,*
it drew you out of the rhythms
of your work. Time and again
you considered how a gourd rattle
could sound like a fistful of pebbles
against stone, or the first patter
of wind-tossed rain, and the clopping
of two rocks together like
aurochs hooves. Depending on
the hand, a skin stretched
on a hoop might be subtle enough
for heartbeats, or the first fisted
rumble of a storm. But with nothing
more than their beaks the birds
made their whoops and *carrocks*
to announce a triumph or ask
sweet questions. So when you came
across the bones of a griffon vulture
on a field, and began to study
its wreckage for useful parts,
I can see you snapping off a likely
section of wing bone and rubbing it
with a chamois rag too far gone to wear,
thinking it over as that bird
among the leaves seemed to be
taunting *See me see me, see see me,*
and instead of sharpening the bone
you split it along both sides
with a flint point, then fit your fingers
to where you'd drill the holes before
you made it one bone again

and tried your breath down its length,
Thweep fee seep me in every variation
but the bird's, though already
children by the fire were pointing
and running to you up the field.

Covey

The first bobwhite runs long-necked
across the road from the river's edge
to the hillside where deer trails
come down to the drinking places,
and there goes another, tall-necked
so I think of girls from a choir
lifting their robes for speed before
imminent rain. Three times
in two weeks I've seen them,
often enough to declare
a resident covey, crucial because
these quail are going the way
the whippoorwills of our childhood
evenings went as the open woods
were parceled off for homes. By the time
I've counted five across the road, I'm at
the spot where they've been foraging
the riverbank's seed hoard and
decembered leaves, not one in sight
though I know from our last
encounter there's at least a dozen more
crouched in place down there—
not all this crackling and whispering's
from the breeze. And now a piper cub
crosses above Cathedral Hill and circles
the river's meandering, perhaps to observe
a man down here stopped and gazing
as though he'd set out walking his route
and come to himself in a new place.

Two for the Old Easy

1. Tree of Paradise

What are the odds of it growing here
in the courtyard: wind hissing
through leaves large as
the tropical canoe paddles
in some South Sea epic,
the stems looking frail enough
for a slant of hailstones
to wreck during this evening's
guaranteed cloud blitz
off the Gulf? To taste of the fruit
you will have to negotiate
with this bud that's dangling purple
like a pod head in front of it,
before you realize it wasn't
an apple or quince in Eden
but a banana, the Tree of Paradise
as the Koran has it. Flashy, yes,
and blatant: this whole fragile
bat-pollinated apparatus
jury-rigged to hang a flower
grown serpentine and discursive from,
first salesman, sophist, demagogue.

2. The Swarm

Like slathered barbecue
forgotten on a grill, reduced
to a cloud of random particles
and driven from bayous across
the mall parking lot,
a sootfall is floating down
on summer-flashed chrome,

and in through sliding doors
on the shoulders of consumers.
Up close there are two
orange heads—each flake
is bugs coupling in air, joined
like dogs but more so, the lovebugs,
connected for days, as if
they knew this city,
under its fake Republic Picture
clouds, is sinking, the streets
buckling at sea level, shifting,
humped each morning in new ways
the seismic cracks in ceilings
complement, and so it's freebies
all around on any bayou road
or Interstate crossing a creek,
and what a way to go!
The windshields pelted with
winged splashes of an ecstasy
no cloudburst will remove.

Two Birds in the Evening

When that oriole whistled from the orchard
it seemed to be frankly asking, *You got*
a problem with that? Its orange and black
was brash as a high-school letter sweater.
No problem, no problem, except it seemed
like Saturday night under the old Rialto's
marquee again. At least until a rubythroat
running a quality-control check
on a trumpetvine drew nearer and I thought,
This is what I'd like next time around,
to be one of the air's accomplices,
too quick for boredom and
acrobatic in love.

Indignities

Coming down to breakfast I saw
in your gape what *rictus* meant,
old dog, and in my own
at your presence flat and stiff
on the kitchen floor.

That was the first indignity,
then how I dragged you
through everything that mattered
and out the door, and fitted you
to my firewood cart, startled

by how flexible you were
in some new places (almost as though
agreeing to the journey), before I could
get you up the path to the car
and refit you there. All the way

to the vet's with windows open,
then onto the stretcher headed for
the ashes, no treats this time
from the vet's aides for Magnus,
the handsome border collie, and no hugs
from the formerly libidinous you.

This afternoon as I was thinking
that Heaven wouldn't be
worthwhile without you, the puppy
was gamboling down the beach

with your favorite ball,
but the final indignity
will be the day I stop stepping
over the places where you were.

Lefty

His eyes cannot believe
what his legs are doing. Off the leash
he is stotting on this winter beach,
springing in place like a lamb, now bucking,
flexing the way years ago I watched
two fawns as they climbed Rose's Hill
ranging against each other in fifteen
minutes of play. Lefty the leftover,
last of his litter, whom I brought home
in trepidation because of that,
though the sheen on his coat
and a brainy light in his eyes
promised that he might learn not to mess
in the wrong places and chew up shoes,
and grow with no hurry into a border collie,
a sheepdog full of agreeable surprises,
who might be like Patches was,
knowing when the blueberries are ripe
and raking an arm of the bush
for a mouthful. I have witnesses to that,
and how if you told Finnbarr it was raining,
he'd return from the door to his denning place
under the coffee table. If his tail swiped
a sheet of paper off that table
he'd pick it off the floor and bring it to me
with a sorry eye, his mouth as useful as
an opposable thumb, and once when I flicked
his nose with a finger in play, he took my hand
as lightly as a nurse might and looked me
in the eye to say, Please don't do that again.

Lefty, Lefticus maximus, Leftospirosis,
McLefcowitz, we have worked our way

around mutual distrust. You were worth
more than one trip up that old cart road
in western Maine, far from the doggie WalMarts
and the shepherd with a B.S. in Nantucket Studies.
If you will give me a throaty hoot after dinner
like Magnus used to, or watch birds out the window
a half-hour at a time, we will do the beach early
for sunups and to flush the occasional fox
from the tall grass, and hear the wing-thresh
of a pair of tundra swans even before
we see them. When I do the math it's clear
you may be my last dog: last night
I couldn't recall who wrote "The Bothie of
Tober-na-Vuolich." Finally it came to me
and I said Arthur Hugh Clough out loud,
glad to have dodged another blown fuse.
You looked up from the rug, your eyes
agreeing, "Yes, that's it. That's it."

Between Two Pine Trunks

What it wasn't
was one of those miniature
electrical storms that can appear
in a corner of the eye.
This one was in blues, greens,
purples, colors exotic as
the jewelry hawked on TV channels
and perhaps with names like
alexandrite and peridot,
though the tones kept changing.

It wasn't in the eye at all,
but a sun-projected hologram
between two pine trunks,
hallucinatory until
I saw that a dragonfly had somehow
impaled itself in a spider's web
finer than any mist net
and vibrating with the fly's
panic and the smaller spider's
apparent delight—it
couldn't believe its luck!

Sun on the gaudy tail
kept varying those colors. But why,
with those polyfaceted eyes,
this conclusion? Up close
the dynamics of creation
are seldom beautiful.

A Note from the Spadefoot Toads

When it seems less like a song
than a drunk hooting gibberish
in a culvert somewhere, stubborn
and unwilling to come clean,
forget the winged horse and remember
us waiting for that first warm April
night rain to blow in waves
from the west and pool
out here in the Province Lands.

Waters shallow and ephemeral
will appear in this vest-pocket Sahara,
and soon where we've hibernated
half the year under sand we burrowed
with the spurs on our hind feet,
the night will be totally ga-ga with us,
hundreds calling for our consorts
on new shores among the dunes.

You'll hear us a half mile away,
drab as brown pebbles but crying
like nothing so much as newly
fledged crows who haven't yet
learned their *karoks* and *yawks*.
These hourglass stripes on our backs
will seem like promises then:
wait and take heart.

We Live in the Largesse of Our Nickle-Dime Moments

Even Adonis, that gored fertility boy
who bled flowers—expected by the underworld's
Shadows to lament the lost Venus Aphrodite—
confessed he missed the sun, stars and moon most,

and since he was a green man, dropped
into mortal life when the trunk
of a myrtle split, added cucumbers,
apples and pears to his losses.

Closer to home, remember Henry Fowler
a month dead, and Mrs. Fowler on her knees
up at the North Cemetery, troweling in
tomato plants before the face of his stone,

and Gerry Kelly buried with a hammer
near his right hand, a carpenter
as Henry was a farmer.

The quotidian is no one's birthright:
If Canada geese, homecoming through
the February dark—their cries at first
like a pack of hounds on the distant
trace of something—wake you smiling,

pay attention next time they drop down
spread-winged over your rooftree to furrow
the marsh pond. Our obituaries
betray no inkling of the things
we will weep for in a coming world.

CPSIA information can be obtained at www.ICGtesting.com
Printed in the USA
BVOW02s1119170415

396551BV00004B/17/P